Cambridge Young Learners English Tests

Cambridge Starters 1

Examination papers from the

University of Cambridge
Local Examinations Syndicate

CAMBRIDGE
UNIVERSITY PRESS

CAMBRIDGE UNIVERSITY PRESS
Cambridge, New York, Melbourne, Madrid, Cape Town, Singapore, São Paulo

Cambridge University Press
The Edinburgh Building, Cambridge CB2 2RU, UK

www.cambridge.org
Information on this title: www.cambridge.org/9780521659048

First published 1999
9th printing 2005

Printed in Dubai by Oriental Press

ISBN-13 978-0-521-65904-8 Student's Book
ISBN-10 0-521-65904-3 Student's Book

ISBN-13 978-0-521-66766-1 Answer Booklet
ISBN-10 0-521-66766-6 Answer Booklet

ISBN-13 978-0-521-65901-7 Cassette
ISBN-10 0-521-65901-9 Cassette

Contents

Part 1

– 5 questions –

Can you see the line between the cat and the bus?
This is an example.
Listen and draw lines.

Part 2
– 5 questions –

Listen and write a name or a number. There are two examples.

Examples:

.... Sam

.... 10

Questions:

1

....

2  ....

3  ....

4  ....

5  ....

Part 3
– 5 questions –

Listen and tick (✔) the box.

<u>Example</u>: What's Bill doing?

  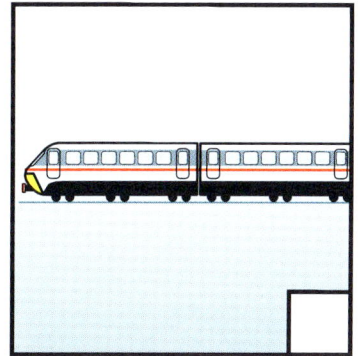

<u>Questions</u>:

1   What's Tom playing?

2   What's Nick doing?

3   What's Ben doing?

4   What's Kim doing?

5   What's Ann painting?

Part 4
– 5 questions –

Listen and colour.

Reading and Writing

Part 1
– 5 questions –

Look and read. Put a tick (✔) or a cross (✗) in the box.

<u>Examples</u>:

This is a camera.

This is a chicken.

<u>Questions</u>:

1

This is a bath.

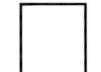

2    This is a snake.   ☐

3    This is a boat.   ☐

4    This is a sock.   ☐

5 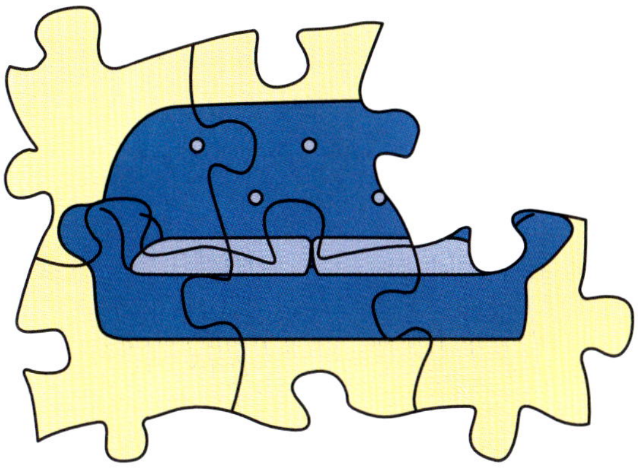   This is a sofa.   ☐

Part 2
– 5 questions –

Look and read. Write yes or no.

Examples:

There is a monster between the girl
and the boy. .... *yes* ....

The monster is eating a pineapple. .... *no* ....

Questions:

1   The boy is fishing. ....

2   There is a fish in the water. ....

3   The girl is drawing a picture. ....

4   The monster is flying a kite. ....

5   The girl is wearing trousers. ....

Part 3
– 5 questions –

Look at the pictures. Look at the letters. Write the words.

<u>Example</u>:

 <u>e</u> <u>a</u> <u>r</u>

<u>Questions</u>:

1  — — — — —

2 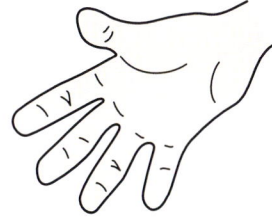 — — — —

3 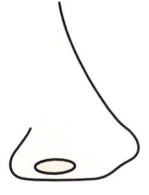 — — — —

4 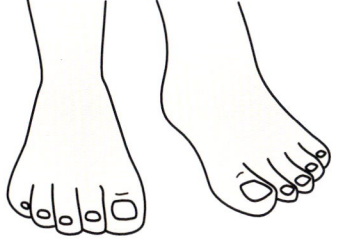 — — — —

5  — — — —

Part 4

– 5 questions –

Read the story. Look at the pictures and the example.
Write one-word answers.

There are ten desks and two .... *chairs* .... in my

classroom. There is a big ....

and a small cupboard next to it. There are some

.... on the cupboard. In the cupboard there

are some .... The teacher stands behind a

big .... She wears a blue skirt

and a white ....

Part 5
– 5 questions –

Look at the pictures and read the questions.
Write one-word answers.

PICTURE A

Examples:

How many bags are there? ....four..................

What is the man eating? a ....banana..................

Questions:

1 What is the boy playing with? a ....

PICTURE B

2   Where are they now?   in a ....

3   How many people can you see?   ....

PICTURE C

4   What are they doing?   ....

5   What is on the man's head?   a ....!

SCENE CARD

OBJECT CARDS

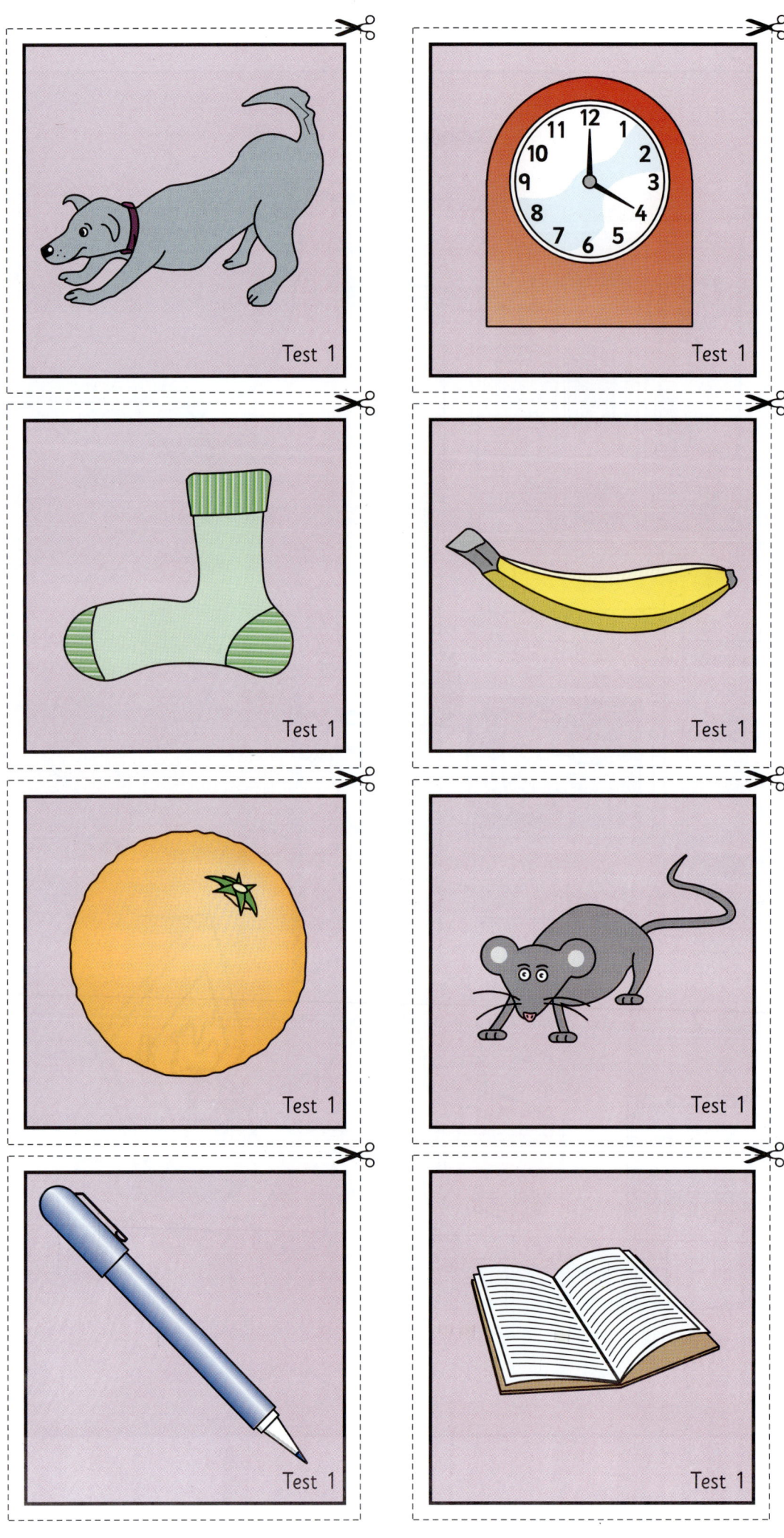

15

Part 1
– 5 questions –

Can you see the line between the orange and the table? This is an example.
Listen and draw lines.

Part 2
– 5 questions –

Listen and write a name or a number. There are two examples.

Examples:

.... Nick ....

.... 3 ....

Questions:

1

....

2

....

3

....

4

.... *Street* ....

? Street

5

....

Part 3

– 5 questions –

Listen and tick (✔) the box.

<u>Example</u>: What's Sue playing with?

<u>Questions</u>:

1   What's Tom doing?

2   Where's Mummy?

3   What's Daddy doing?

4   What game are Sam and Pat playing?

5   What's Grandfather doing?

Part 4
– 5 questions –

Listen and colour.

Reading and Writing

Part 1
– 5 questions –

Look and read. Put a tick (✔) or a cross (✗) in the box.

<u>Examples</u>:

This is a plane.

This is a dog.

<u>Questions</u>:

1

This is a flower.

2

This is a camera. ☐

3

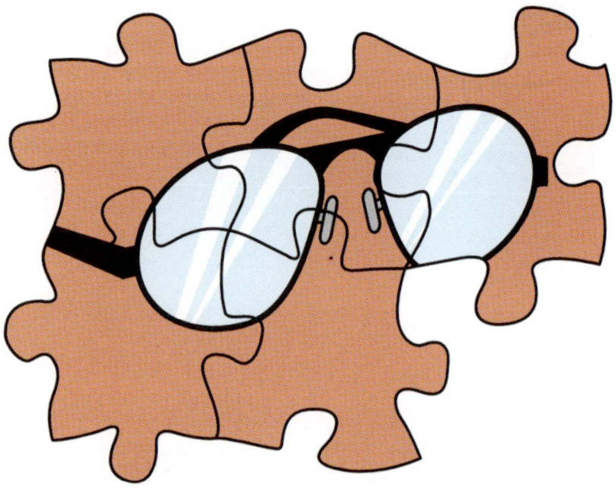

This is a mirror. ☐

4

This is a boat. ☐

5

This is a cow. ☐

Part 2
– 5 questions –

Look and read. Write yes or no.

Examples:

There is a cake on the table. ....yes...........

The mouse is under the chair. ....no...........

Questions:

1   The boy is sitting at the table. ....

2   There is an elephant in the cupboard. ....

3   The boy is wearing a blue shirt. ....

4   The girl is playing the piano. ....

5   The lamp is between the cupboard
    and the picture. ....

Part 3
– 5 questions –

Look at the pictures. Look at the letters. Write the words.

<u>Example</u>:

s o c c e r

<u>Questions</u>:

1 _ _ _ _ _ _

2 _ _ _ _ _ _

3 _ _ _ _ _ _ _ _

4 _ _ _ _ _ _ _

5 _ _ _ _

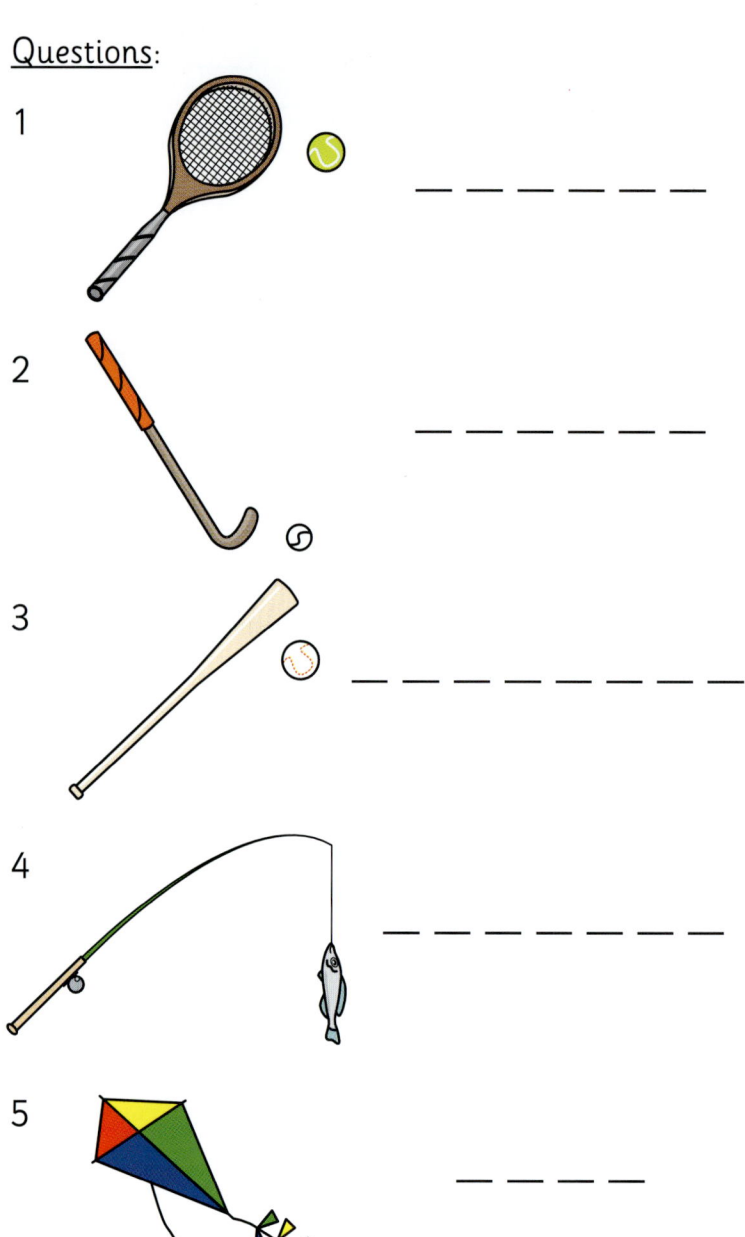

Part 4
– 5 questions –

**Read the story. Look at the pictures and the example.
Write one-word answers.**

What am I?

I live in a .... *house* .... You can find me in a

living room, a kitchen or a .... I am like a big

or small box. My picture is .... and white or colour.

Families watch sports like .... or basketball on me.

I show pictures of men and women, houses, animals and

....

What am I?

I'm a __ __ !

26

Part 5
– 5 questions –

Look at the pictures and read the questions.
Write one-word answers.

PICTURE A

Examples:

What is the woman wearing on her head?   a .... hat ....

How many men are there?   .... three ....

Questions:

1   What colour is the girl's hair?   ....

PICTURE B

2   How many tigers are there?   ....

3   What are they doing?   ....

PICTURE C

4   Where is the girl?   in a   ....

5   What are the tigers eating?   ....

SCENE CARD

OBJECT CARDS

Test 2

Test 2

Test 2

Test 2

Test 2

Test 2

Test 2

Test 2

Listening

Part 1
– 5 questions –

Can you see the line between the duck and the bath? This is an example.
Listen and draw lines.

Part 2
– 5 questions –

Listen and write a name or a number. There are two examples.

Examples:

.... May

.... 8

Questions:

1

....

2

....

3

....

4

....

5

.... Street

Part 3
– 5 questions –

Listen and tick (✔) the box.

<u>Example</u>: What's Tom doing?

<u>Questions</u>:

1   What's Sue doing?

2   Where are the children?

3   What's the teacher doing?

4   What are the girls eating?

5   What game are the boys playing?

Part 4
– 5 questions –

Listen and colour.

Reading and Writing

Part 1
– 5 questions –

Look and read. Put a tick (✔) or a cross (✗) in the box.

Examples:

This is a baby.

This is a boat.

Questions:

1

This is a motorbike.

2   This is a lamp.   ☐

3   This is an eraser.   ☐

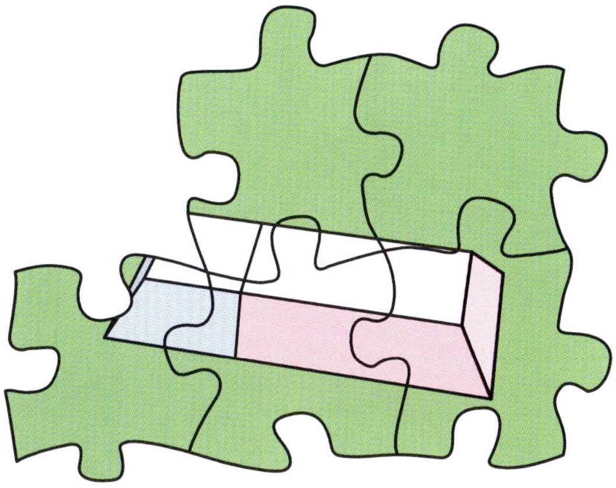

4   This is a door.   ☐

5   This is a ruler.   ☐

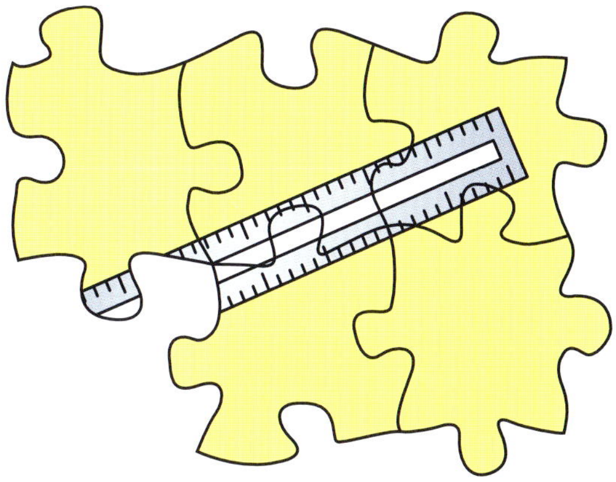

Part 2
– 5 questions –

Look and read. Write yes or no.

Examples:

The girl is reading a book.	*yes*
There is a lizard on the mat.	*no*

Questions:

1　The boy is sitting in an armchair. ....

2　The frog has got a guitar. ....

3　There is a doll on the television. ....

4　The cat is under the sofa. ....

5　The girl is wearing purple shoes. ....

Part 3
– 5 questions –

Look at the pictures. Look at the letters. Write the words.

Example:

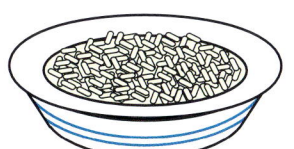   <u>r</u> <u>i</u> <u>c</u> <u>e</u>

Questions:

1      – – – – – –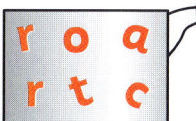

2      – – – – –

3   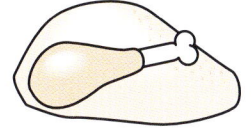   – – – – – – –

4      – – – – – –

5   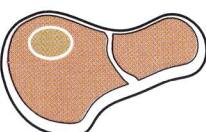   – – – –

Part 4

– 5 questions –

Read the story. Look at the pictures and the example. Write one-word answers.

<u>What am I?</u>

You can find me in the ....*house*............ .

Men have me in their .... Women put

me in their .... Children take me to school.

They draw beautiful pictures of .... and flowers

with me, or write words and sentences for their teachers.

I am .... or black or red or green.

What am I?

I'm a __ __ __ __ __ __ !

41

Part 5
– 5 questions –

**Look at the pictures and read the questions.
Write one-word answers.**

PICTURE A

Examples:

How many animals are there? .... five ....

Where is the hippo? in the .... water ....

Questions:

1   What is the duck doing? ....

PICTURE B

2   How many monkeys are there?   . . . .

3   What are they playing with?   *a*   . . . .

PICTURE C

4   What is the girl doing?   . . . .

5   What is the monkey eating?   *an*   . . . .

Speaking

SCENE CARD